Tools
For
Bible Teachers

Be diligent in these matters; give yourself wholly to them, so that everyone may see your progress.
(1 Timothy 4:15)

Dr. Charles R. Vogan Jr.

Copyright © 1997 Charles R. Vogan Jr.
All rights reserved

Scripture taken from the HOLY BIBLE, NEW INTERNATIONAL VERSION, Copyright © 1973, 1978, 1984 International Bible Society. Used by permission of Zondervan Bible Publishers.

ISBN 978-0-6151-3929-6

Ravenbrook Publishers

A subsidiary of
Shenandoah Bible Ministries

www.shenbible.org

Contents

The Purpose of Tools	5
The Needs of Your Students	8
The Gift of Teaching	15
The Tools for Teaching the Bible	19
Prayer	19
The Bible	24
A Method	37
Bible Study Helps	511
Think	63
Judge the Results	76

Other titles by the same author …

Mystery Revealed: A Beginner's Bible Survey

The Secret to Answered Prayer

Profitable Servants

The Bible Explains Creation

Ten Keys To The Bible

Knots Untied

Teaching Children About Jesus

The Ways Of The Lord

The Works Of The Lord

The Witness

Eight Fundamentals of the Christian Faith

Where the Paths Meet

What the Bible Says About Hell

What the Bible Says About Heaven

The Purpose of Tools

Man is a tool-user. He differs from the animals in the kind of brain that he has – a brain that can see the problem and devise a tool to solve the problem. If he needs to travel, he saves energy by building a wheeled vehicle to take him where he wants to go. If he needs to communicate, he builds a system of telephones and computers to transmit his thoughts wherever in the world he wishes. Because of his ability to build tools he can accomplish an enormous amount of work. Without tools, he's almost as helpless as the dumb animals who have to rely, largely, on chance and physical prowess.

There are also tools that can help us teach the Bible. You may not have thought about this much, but getting people to hear and believe God's truth is the hardest task a teacher can face. It doesn't take much to convince a student about the benefits of math, nor even to teach him how to use it. But when it comes to the Bible, the sinfulness of man and his natural rebellion present the teacher with an almost insurmountable barrier that it takes the Spirit of God to break through.

You probably have experienced the frustration of not being able to get through to your students. And a

The Purpose of Tools

large part of that frustration may come from the fact that you really don't know how to present the material clearly, or convincingly. Maybe you barely know this material yourself! In any case, it's time you become familiar with effective tools that will lay the Bible out before your students in such a clear light that they can't help but see God and hear him speaking to them. When you've taken advantage of the opportunity that these tools give you, *then* you can say that you've done your part – that you've done all that you can do for your students.

Tools can be complex at times. It takes special training to learn to use tools. I'm sure most of us wouldn't know how to operate an electron microscope without a good deal of training! The same goes for God's Word, which is, by the way, the most complex and profound textbook that a teacher has ever attempted to teach. The tools for teaching it are powerful, but it shouldn't come as any surprise that they are also complex – that it will take a lot of training and skill to use them.

The tools that we have available to us are things that probably you've already heard about, and perhaps you are already using them to some extent. What I wish to do here is hold up the potential in each of them so that you can appreciate just how powerful they really are. God gave us tools that will help us accomplish the impossible – which in this dark generation that we live in now, is exactly what we need to win the war:

The weapons we fight with are not the weapons of the world. On the contrary, they have divine power to demolish strongholds. We demolish arguments and every pretension that sets itself up against the knowledge of God, and we take captive

The Purpose of Tools

every thought to make it obedient to Christ. *(2 Corinthians 10:4-5)*

The teacher of the Bible has to focus on the "one thing needful." Students can get a lot of understanding about how the world works from secular schools, but in order to fill the aching void in their souls they have only one place to turn – the Bible. ***You are the one sent to help fill that void.*** Your challenge is to get eternal truth into their heads and hearts, and make them see it so clearly that their lives will change as a result. You need something to touch the conscience that's suffering under the pain of sin; you need something to give hope to the dying; you need something to open blind spiritual eyes so that they can see a risen Savior in Heaven. The tools of a teacher, in other words, are doing the impossible: they are going far beyond the limited scope of man's so-called "helps" that have failed to deliver people from sin and death in the past.

Since you have such a big job on your hands, the first thing you need to do is learn the tools of the trade.

The Needs of your Students

As you stand in front of your students, if you care for them at all, you're no doubt going to ask yourself – can I give them what they need? But in order to do that, you're going to have to *know* what they need; they often don't know themselves!

Modern teachers often make the mistake of *assuming* what their students need without finding out from the Bible what people *really* need. Or worse yet, they don't even think about what their students need – they just blindly accept what their "canned" material gives them and pass it on to their students without questioning whether it's spiritually appropriate.

We mustn't make the mistake of *asking* our students what they think they need – sinners will always respond with "more promises and less responsibility!" Go to God and ask *him* what your students need. He knows: he's interested in righteousness and life. He knows where we all fail, and he knows how to put us together again. With him everything is plain to see. Jesus first handed the loaves and fish to his disciples before he told them, "You go feed them." We must also do the same – we have to go to the Lord and ask him for the right food for our students. Otherwise how useful

The needs of your students

will we be to them? Can our students trust us to give them the "Word of life?"

We can often figure out what our problems must be – and therefore our needs – by carefully studying God's gifts. He fits the answer to the problem; his medicine is designed to heal particular illnesses. For instance, here are a few of God's solutions that fix our problems:

God's Word is authority. When God speaks, he does so with authority and finality. He doesn't apologize for interrupting our thoughts! He expects us to forget about our man-made systems of "truth," to *listen* to him, to learn, and to submit.

> Also check out these passages:
>
> • Matthew 13:1-9
> • Matthew 25

This is because what God says is the *truth*. It's the only way to look at things. We might have opinions of our own, but none of our opinions have ever helped the situation so far – and now it's time to listen to the Creator. He has a perspective that others don't have. He can see the end from the beginning (Isaiah 46:10); he knows us well because he made us. In fact, when God speaks, he not only assumes that we'll pay attention and learn from him, he is going to use this same truth against us on Judgment Day – he will expect us to show a profit from the knowledge that we got from him! How many people will be able to prove that they took his Word seriously? Do people even realize that, since they've now heard his Word, they are responsible eternally for what they've heard? Will they be able to show a profit from what they've heard?

You can't miss the meaning of the Bible unless you're being willfully rebellious. It has

The needs of your students

its complex passages, its difficult ideas; but it also has enough plain and simple teaching that all of us can easily understand and obey – if we were so inclined. Most people *refuse* to understand it – *that's* their root problem with the Bible. It's a matter of authority with them, and they won't be ruled by anybody – not even by God.

So when people won't even look inside the Bible or listen to a teacher present the Bible's claims, you can tell what their problems are: **first,** they have their own standard for living and they don't want to use God's standards. **Second,** they don't understand what it means to be God's servant – a servant listens to his Master and does what his Master expects of him. **Third,** they don't know what it means to glorify and honor God – otherwise they would take his Word as the truth it is and obey it. **Fourth,** they aren't interested in building the Kingdom of God; they much prefer to work on their own kingdoms in this world.

As you can see, the needs are great. You have to literally shift people's allegiance away from themselves to God, to get them to change from rebels to willing servants of God. And you'll have to do this God's way – because only his ways will be effective enough to reach the heart where the real problems lie. This is going to take time and a great deal of spiritual skill.

Take reliance off self and live in faith. The Bible is revelation – which means that it opens God and his world to our eyes so that we can see what was formerly hidden.

The needs of your students

"I tell you the truth, no one can see the Kingdom of God unless he is born again." (John 3:3)

The reason this is necessary is because every one of us were born spiritually blind, completely unable to see God or anything of a spiritual nature. Our five senses only operate on this physical world that we're a part of; we're hopelessly dead, spiritually, to God's spiritual world. We are quite literally dead to God.

That's why we get so much wrong in our lives – and usually we have no idea that we're even offending God with what we do! The newspapers show us just how perverted mankind is, though we all live in God's earth and breathe his air and enjoy his daily blessings. We rebel against his plain Word, without even the desire to know about the Law that we're breaking. Though we've put together some sort of "ethics" or "morality" to make our consciences feel better, actually we haven't even begun to plumb the spiritual depth of God's morality. Judgment Day will show up our shallow religion for what it really is.

Naturally, in such a situation, sin and death is all we can expect out of life. It's no wonder that people's lives are falling apart, that they have so many unsolvable problems and nowhere to turn for help.

The answer for these great needs is faith. Faith is living in the light of God's world. Like a bright searchlight shining down from Heaven, the Spirit of God illuminates our lives with the reality of God – and we can now see what we were formerly blind to. Now we can see who God is, and what he's really like.

The needs of your students

Now we can see what's in our hearts and why our salvation is such a great need. Now we can clearly see the world around us, and the need for avoiding so much of it. We can also see the crying spiritual needs in a fallen and suffering world. The person who lives by faith has eyes in his head: he can see so much that others can't see.

The teacher (and this is humbling to consider) is instrumental in getting this kind of faith into the student. By God's design, hearing the Word produces faith.

How, then, can they call on the one they have not believed in? And how can they believe in the one of whom they have not heard? And how can they hear without someone preaching to them? And how can they preach unless they are sent? (Romans 10:14-15)

To see the fullness of Christ. God is so big, so huge, so complex, that we will never know the full extent of his wisdom and power. But in a dark and fallen world, he also seems so far away from us that we could easily despair that he even cares, let alone the possibility that he could or would help us in our trouble.

But the Lord wants to save us – that's his nature, the root of all his actions toward us. And in the supreme effort to convince us of his goodwill toward his children, he put his entire being and fullness into his Son Jesus Christ:

The needs of your students

 **For God was pleased to have all his fullness dwell in him. (Colossians 1:19)**

The reason this is so significant is that Jesus came among us as one of us. He became man – and therefore came within our reach. We can touch him, hear him, walk with him. He's one of us – we can understand him easily. So now we know God's real feelings toward us.

"That which was from the beginning, which we have heard, which we have seen with our eyes, which we have looked at and our hands have touched – this we proclaim concerning the Word of Life." (1 John 1:1)

Jesus told us many things about his mission in this world, things that ought to encourage the most wayward sinner and the poor soul in the deepest despair. He came to save sinners, he came to seek and save the lost, he rescued the adulteress, he made the blind see and the lame walk. His entire purpose was to help the helpless and bring back the wayward sheep into the fold – all at no cost to them. In this he shows us the true heart of God – a God whom we were prone to think had forgotten about us.

Furthermore, Jesus shows us what God intends to do for us in the future. Since we become one with him, we will get what he got – resurrection, rising above this world over all sin and death, a place at God's right hand, an inheritance as sons. All this is ours because Jesus bought it for us.

The job at hand, however, is to turn the hearts and minds of our students to this Man. He is quite literally our lifeline to all the riches and treasures that God has for us. It's with good reason that Jesus said –

The needs of your students

I am the Way, the Truth, and the Light. No one comes to the Father except through me.
(John 14:6)

If we miss him, we miss it all. If we believe in him and follow him, we have it all. It's like trying to find a narrow road in a bewildering complex of highways and alleyways. Only those who find and walk the "straight and narrow" road will find life. Your job as the teacher is to aim them in the right direction.

These are just a few examples of exploring the needs of your students. I would counsel you to do some serious searching in God's Word and find out the issues that the Lord wants to address in your life as well as theirs. It will help you tremendously in focusing your lessons on matters that are really important, not on the side issues that people love to jump into. Like a mother who provides her family with the essentials of a balanced diet, the teacher of the Bible will be careful to address the eternal needs of the soul.

The Gift of Teaching

Teaching requires skill, but teaching in God's Kingdom needs more than just skill. The Bible tells us that it's one of the special gifts that Christ has given to his Church:

It was he who gave some to be apostles, some to be prophets, some to be evangelists, and some to be pastors and teachers, to prepare God's people for works of service, so that the body of Christ may be built up until we all reach unity in the faith and in the knowledge of the Son of God and become mature, attaining to the whole measure of the fullness of Christ. *(Ephesians 4:11-13)*

Now there are several points to observe in this passage:

First, teaching isn't a matter of volunteerism. So much of Church activity in our day relies on well-meaning, but unskilled, volunteers. God can no more afford to hand over this critical work to unskilled labor than we can assign a plumber to get men to the moon! The Kingdom of God is of such a nature that working on it requires an uncommon wisdom and spiritual discernment;

The Gift of Teaching

otherwise the thing not only won't get done right, we can hurt a lot of people in the process.

Though people show that their hearts are right when they want to help, it often hurts the process to let ignorance and willfulness rule in the classroom. Think about it: for some reason we are careful to get an expert to teach our children physics or math, but we don't seem to care at all about letting someone who knows almost nothing about the Bible teach the profound wisdom of God to our children! And this practice is especially tragic in light of the fact that their souls, their very eternity, hang in the balance!

> Also check out these passages:
> - Matthew 4:18- 22
> - John 15:16

Jesus chose his disciples. He knew what lay ahead, he knew the qualifications necessary for the kind of job he was sending them to do. They didn't know any of this! Peter, remember, kept thinking that he knew what was going on, and he wasn't bashful about "instructing" the Lord about what he ought to do! But he really *didn't* know what was coming, nor what it would take to do the job. So Jesus carefully trained them for at least three years before sending them out to preach the Gospel – and, for most of them, persecution and death because of the Gospel.

> *"He was not seen by all the people, but by <u>witnesses whom God had already chosen ...</u>"*
> *(Acts 10:41)*

No, God is going to hand-pick his own workers and train them himself in his Word and ways. He wants *experts* to lead his people; he wants to make sure his workers are spiritually skilled to build the *right kind* of Kingdom on earth. Knowing this, however, we don't mean to discourage those who want to teach – Paul says that we should earnestly desire spiritual gifts, including that of teaching. But every teacher should say with Paul, "Who is equal to such a task?" (2 Corinthians 2:16) We just have to plead with the Master that he would choose us, call us, and equip us to go out with his blessing and "reap a harvest." "Ask the Lord of the

The Gift of Teaching

harvest, therefore, to send out workers into his harvest field." (Luke 10:2)

Second, God gives this gift. It comes from Heaven, not from the will of man or the training of even the best schools. Though schools and books and education sharpen the skill and hone the edge to give a better cut, nobody but the Creator can make us into a sword in the first place. Some of us are better fitted for other kinds of work in the Church – and it's a mercy when we are enabled to see that. "Not many of you should presume to be teachers, my brothers, because you know that we who teach will be judged more strictly." (James 3:1) Just as Aaron and his descendents couldn't make themselves priests – it was God's assignment, not man's (Hebrews 5:4) – in the same way, teachers are ordinary people whom God calls and equips for a special work.

> Remember King Uzziah, who unlawfully assumed the role of a priest and was immediately inflicted with leprosy!

How do we know we have this gift? There is an easy test; it involves the meaning of spiritual gifts in general. A spiritual gift is *the ability to make Christ more plain to a person*, so that they can see him better and put their faith and trust in him for what he does. All spiritual gifts aim for this – because this is the work of the Holy Spirit among us: to glorify the Lord.

Now if, when you share your study and insight into the Word of God with someone, they end up getting a clearer picture and stronger faith in the Lord Jesus Christ (both from the Old and the New Testament), then you have the gift of teaching. And if this is what happens when you teach – that your students get a bigger picture of God – then you can attribute that gift to the Father who is helping you do something you could never do on your own.

Third, the gift is for a reason: to build God's Kingdom. Christians need work done upon them, just

The Gift of Teaching

like a building under construction. Someone has to know how to lay the foundation, how to lay the brick and stone to construct a wall, how to join the walls and roof, and how to add the finishing touches. Believers in a church need help to see their God, how to walk before him, how to honor him in a dark world, what to do for their brothers and sisters – in short, how to live in God's Kingdom. The teacher opens their eyes to these realities and shows them the work at hand to be done. The teacher succeeds – he/she shows that they truly understand the job at hand – when Christians finally act like what they are – the chosen People of God.

Spiritual Gifts

Apostles
Pastors
Evangelists
Faith
Miracles
Tongues
Prophecy
Message of Knowledge
Administration
Encouraging
Leadership
Teachers
Message of wisdom
Distinguishing spirits
Interpreting tongues
Helping others
Healing
Serving
Contributing to others' needs
Showing mercy

The Tools for Teaching the Bible

Prayer

It goes without saying that a teacher of the Bible first needs to pray. Without God's help, wisdom and strength, you can't hope to know the truth yourself, or get it across to your students. Teaching is such a spiritual exercise that we need spiritual power to accomplish it – and that can come only from Heaven.

Why do we pray?

First, this is God's business that we're involved in, not our own. We are helping him build a spiritual Temple, an eternal Kingdom, a house for him to live in. We are privileged to assist him in this amazing project; but we mustn't make the mistake of trying to take it out of his hands and do our own thing. He already laid out his plans before the world began. He knows what he's doing, he knows why he wants things done a certain

"You also, like living stones, are being built into a spiritual house ..."
(1 Peter 2:5)

way, and the only thing he wants from us is cooperation.

Prayer is like looking over his shoulders at the blueprints he made for his house. As long as it's his name signed down in the corner of the prints, we had better learn to put aside our own "kingdom" and get busy working on his instead.

The Israelites learned the priorities of God's kingdom when they came back from the Exile. Looking over Jerusalem lying in ruins, they figured that the first priority was to build themselves nice homes. Not so!

> **"Is it a time for you yourselves to be living in your paneled houses, while this house remains a ruin?" ... Go up into the mountains and bring down timber and build the house, so that I may take pleasure in it and be honored," says the LORD. "You expected much, but see, it turned out to be little. What you brought home, I blew away. Why?" declares the LORD Almighty. "Because of my house, which remains a ruin, while each of you is busy with his own house."**
> **(Haggai 1:4, 8-9)**

Six Essentials of Prayer

- Pray according to the Word
- Start with God's Name
- Pray in the Spirit
- Pray with faith
- Pray for his will
- Pray for his glory

It would be a shame if you were determined to do your own thing, and when you prayed you just informed God what you were going to do and expected him to "bless" your work. You will eventually find that this results not in spiritual success but miserable failure. You will find yourself

The Tools for teaching the Bible - Prayer

alone, with more problems than you can solve, with nobody on your side – least of all God! – and nowhere to turn for help.

You can't argue with success, or the lack of it. If you and the Lord are working on the same thing, things go remarkably well – because God can't fail. But if you and he aren't working on the same things, your work won't measure up to his standards on the last day.

> **Unless the LORD builds the house,**
> **its builders labor in vain.**
> **Unless the LORD watches over the city,**
> **the watchmen stand guard in vain.**
> **(Psalm 127:1)**

Second, our work involves spiritual materials that we aren't naturally equipped to handle. Don't forget that you are called to work on a *spiritual* kingdom – do you know where to start? Do you know what materials to use? Do you know how to fit things together? It isn't like working on an earthly project or building! This requires insight into a spiritual world that can only come from the Spirit working in our minds and hearts.

Third, when you pray, you aren't so much asking (or telling!) God what to do so much as you are getting orders from him. We often forget that he is the Lord, the Master, the Almighty before whom all must bend their knees. We forget that he already knows "the end from the beginning," and he doesn't need us to fill him in on any details. *We* are the ones who are in the fog, who can't see

> *"Go near to listen rather than to offer the sacrifice of fools ..."*
> *(Ecclesiastes 5:1)*

the road ahead of us because we are just finite creatures.

You've no doubt heard the saying, "prayer changes things." I'd like to change that a little bit and say that "prayer changes *you*." If you come to God with a heart of humility, with a quiet and gentle spirit, ready to listen and not just blab away whatever comes into your head – he'll be more inclined to hear your requests and let you in on what he intends to do in your life. Picture it as a servant coming to the Master for the orders of the day: you know what you need to do (generally speaking), and you know that you need a great deal of wisdom and strength from God to accomplish it. Appear before his throne willing to do the work his way, and accept from him his promises and help and plans for carrying out your duties, and things will go much better for you in your work.

> *The apostles knew how to pray to get answers – see Acts 4:24-31*

When you pray, you need to focus on **answers**. Prayer without answers is a waste of everyone's time. Modern Christians almost expect that their prayers will go unanswered – maybe because they don't have the faith in God to actually give them what they need! A conversation between two people consists of two-way communication; if only one is talking, it isn't a conversation but a monologue. God has given us many promises that he will answer our prayers, if only we come to him believing that he will.

You *need* answers to prayer. You need a clear idea of God's Word, which is the most difficult book in print for man to understand. Your students need help from you, not just games and stories that don't touch the heart and change their lives. You need results from your

The Tools for teaching the Bible - Prayer

teaching, results that you can show the Master at the end of time. He's a hard master, remember (Luke 19:22), and he expects measurable results from your work. If he wants this kind of success from your teaching, then learn a lesson from Jacob and struggle with God until he blesses you with the answers you need.

Does the Lord talk to his people? Most definitely! But it takes a keen ear and some experience in spiritual matters. He doesn't hang signs down from Heaven, and usually he doesn't send someone along with the answers for your questions. He will sometimes speak to you through circumstances. For instance, when your students hardly know the first thing about the Bible stories, you can safely assume that the Lord wants you to work on the basics of the faith. You'd be closing your eyes to the obvious if you insisted on teaching adult-level material to "babes in the faith."

"In the past God spoke to our forefathers through the prophets at many times and in various ways, but in these last days he has spoken to us by his Son ..." (Hebrews 1:1-2)

But he mainly answers prayer through his Word. The answer to all of life's problems are in the Bible; you just have to learn how to listen when God speaks to you there. Some people will simply open the Bible randomly and read what they find, thinking that this is how God teaches them. That rarely works out well, however. A more certain approach is to start learning the important passages of the Bible so well that, when the time comes to talk to God about important matters, familiar passages will come to mind and give you the direction you're looking for. Many times I've prayed and prayed over a matter, and then one day while I'm studying a certain passage the answer I've been looking for jumps out at me! For the person who constantly has his/her "spiritual antennae" up while studying the Bible, answers to prayer come constantly and in season.

The Bible

There are a lot of teachers that depend completely on a Sunday School quarterly, or some pre-programmed material for their lesson plans. Perhaps they don't feel comfortable teaching from the Bible itself – perhaps they don't know enough about it to make adequate lessons, and they feel that it's OK to depend on the work of specialists. The problems with this approach are these:

First, a teacher who claims to teach the Bible, and yet can't use the Bible itself as a primary textbook, really doesn't know what he's talking about and shouldn't claim to have any expertise in the Bible. Nor should others have to submit themselves to his lack of knowledge. Students in secular schools want to sit at the feet of experts, not "teachers" who can only read the lessons that someone else has already written out for them.

Second, it puts the focus of the lesson on the quarterly, not on the Bible. So what happens is that the students don't get any familiarity with the Bible either. What started out as a teacher who doesn't feel comfortable working out of the Bible results in an entire classroom of students who will never feel comfortable with it. The problem gets multiplied many times over in short order.

I know that training teachers to get comfortable and skillful at teaching the Bible requires a lot of time and resources, and since churches operate on tight budgets (unlike businesses who can afford to pay for

The Tools for teaching the Bible - The Bible

training their employees) then the problem isn't likely to get solved very soon. But for that reason, the burden of changing the way the system works may fall on the conscientious teacher. Perhaps out of love for his students, and fear of God whom he serves, he ought to take the time to get skilled at working with the Bible. After all, *he's* going to be the one judged for the results – or lack of them! In the end it's his responsibility to master the book and teach it.

The Bible is a textbook, no less than those used in secular schools. It has information that students need to learn. Somehow you need to be able to master the book yourself so that you can lead your students into its pages. You're going to have beginning, intermediate, and advanced students – can you put together meaningful lessons from the Bible for each type of student? You need to be able to make lesson plans, outlines, book surveys, biographical and geographical studies. You'll need to know where to point students who are looking for specific subjects. You'll have to know some Biblical history. You'll have to learn how to apply the Bible's lessons so that it won't just be an intellectual exercise, but what it really is – orders from Heaven for God's children to carry out. This is a big enterprise that you've entered into!

In order to be that proficient with the Bible, you'll have to familiarize yourself with its teaching. There are many useful books on Bible doctrine, and its basic teaching, that will help you get started. But personally I like to back way up and see the forest for the trees. If I can see the plan of the entire book, that will help me understand smaller parts of it. I can keep that overall picture in mind as I study individual passages, and it will keep me from going off into wrong interpretations. Since everything in the Bible fits together, seeing the overall picture will help me look for, and form, the links between the smaller parts.

Here is a sample of what I mean. When I backed up far enough to see the entire sweep of the Old Testament, this is what I saw it teaching me:

The Old Testament reveals Christ and our relationship to the Father through him.

In other words, the Old Testament uses many methods to completely "unpack" the full story of Christ for us. This may come as a surprise for Christians, who thought the news about Christ was pretty much limited to the New Testament! But really the Lord had the person and work of Christ in mind "from the beginning of the world." It was all carefully planned out at the start. Everything in the Old Testament fit into the plan of God's Messiah.

The Jews during Old Testament times missed the point, of course, because they were too close to the events to see what was going on overall, and they refused to listen to the Prophets who described the whole thing to them.

When Paul explained the Gospel to the Jews in the New Testament, he used the Old Testament to do it – that was his textbook that he used in evangelizing the nations.

... the holy Scriptures, which are able to make you wise for salvation through faith in Christ Jesus. (2 Timothy 3:15)

The Tools for teaching the Bible - The Bible

And the New Testament, if you examine it closely, felt that the Old Testament did an excellent job at describing Christ – so much so that it doesn't go over the material again. It moves the student on to higher levels of understanding; but the whole time it assumes that you've already done your homework in the OT. What that means, of course, is that if you haven't done your homework, you'll miss out on many essential truths about Christ!

When I backed up enough to see the scope of the New Testament, this is what I found:

The New Testament reveals the New Man and how we become one with him.

See Ephesians 1 for a full description of what God has in mind for us

In other words, the New Testament tells us of a *new thing*: what God intended to do with his children throughout eternity. He wanted us to live forever, to be pure of sin to such a degree that the Law would be completely satisfied, to enjoy the riches and treasures of Heaven, to know him in such a way that we literally will live from his hands and no longer have to receive blessings from him through created means.

The way he chose to bring us into this inheritance is to make us one with his Son Jesus Christ – who himself experienced the full extent of God's plans for his children. Christ is the first-born Son, who was the first to rise from the dead into the life that God has for his family. And when we become one with him, we take on his characteristics, his life, his eternity – we share the fullness of his life.

The Tools for teaching the Bible - The Bible

Now take these two insights back to the Bible and you will keep a proper perspective on whatever you learn there.

There is also a list of **Ten Keys** that I've distilled from all my studies of the Bible. These "keys" are principles that span the entire Bible, from beginning to end. They are there in every passage. If you know what these keys are, you can use them to unlock the meaning of any passage of the Bible – Old or New Testament. Here are the Keys:

Ten Keys
Revelation
Miracle
Ways
Works
Glory
Faith
Name
Prophecy
Deliverance
Covenant

• **The Bible reveals God** – The entire Bible uncovers the hidden mystery of the true nature of God and what he does in our world. It also reveals our hearts and our relationship to God – and how he restores what we lost at Creation.

• **God works miracles** – Since we need more than this created world can give us to solve our problems of sin and death, God responds by giving us what only he can give – answers from Heaven. His power always does the impossible.

• **God has ways** – God likes to go about things in certain ways, and he expects us to know what those ways are so that we can work with him, not against him. His ways are not our ways of doing things – but they are the ways of life.

• **God has special works** – God does things that no other being can claim to do. The reason this is important is that only his works last, only his works can save us. Our works can do nothing to save us. Those who know what God's works are will be able to take advantage of that knowledge.

• **God demands glory** – God must get all credit for what he does, which is what the word "glory" really means. And he demands glory for this reason: that people will finally know who the real King is, who the real Savior is, and turn to him when they need help.

• **Faith lives in the light of God's world** – The Spirit of God shines light down from Heaven on those who walk in faith. They can see what others can't see – the true nature of God, themselves, the world they live in. We need to be able to see like this if we hope to reach our goal in Heaven!

• **God's Names describe him** – God graciously gave us a way of understanding his unending and complex nature: his Names. If we study his Names carefully (especially the Name described in Exodus 34:6-7), we will know which God we're praying to and call on him by his proper Name. We will also know what to ask for and expect from this God.

• **Prophecy reveals the coming Kingdom of God** – The Lord is coming with an army to put down rebels in this world, destroy the kingdom of the devil, and set up his own Kingdom in its place – a Kingdom of life and peace and righteousness. Prophets are messengers sent ahead of the Lord's coming to warn us of what's about to happen: repent *now*, and switch sides, before it's too late!

- **Deliverance is getting someone out of danger, into a safe place** – The Lord specializes in getting people out of trouble. He does that by miraculously lifting them out of the mess and putting them in a safe place. Anything short of that isn't deliverance: we can't claim to be saved if we haven't been removed from danger!

- **The basis of God's grace to us is the covenant of Abraham** – When God made a covenant with Abraham, he laid out the terms of what he intends to do for Abraham and all his children. Those terms still hold true today: Christians receive the covenant blessings from God because they have the faith of their father Abraham.

Summary: All this is to get you started on learning the truths of the Bible – not in a superficial way, but a fundamental and powerful way. The teacher of the Bible has to be the master of his subject – these points provide the necessary "coursework" to become a Master Teacher.

The Bible is such a powerful tool to use in getting truth across to your students that you should do whatever necessary to become master of it. Here are several steps that you can use to get a better grasp on the book yourself:

- *Look at what it says* – Probably the biggest mistake that people make when they study the Bible is that they run away before they're done. They read it for a few minutes, decide that they know what it's saying, and then close the book. Besides the fact that they aren't going to get down deep to the root meaning, they are probably going to read their own ideas into the text – ideas that aren't really there. In other words, because of what they *already* believe, they can't see what it really says.

For example, one of the most misunderstood passages of all time has to be Isaiah 28:9-13. The Hebrew reads thus: "sav lasav, sav lasav, kav lakav, kav lakav." (The NIV makes note of this in a footnote.) These words mean absolutely nothing! They are gibberish that the prophet is imitating – they could just as easily be translated, "la de da, la de da!"

However, most translators, unfortunately, try to put these nonsense syllables into some meaningful form of English for the sake of the reader. You've probably heard the King James translation of this verse – "precept upon precept, line upon line." This makes this passage say what it most definitely does *not* say! Instead of looking at the Hebrew original, people go with the KJV and claim that it refers to the building blocks of faith – that we grow in understanding through learning a little bit at a time until we are mature in the faith.

But the context is the exact opposite! If you would read the bigger passage carefully (back up to the beginning of the chapter!), this is what you'll find going on: The prophet was forced to deal with the Israelites

> *Another good example is in 1 Corinthians 8 – many claim that it teaches that "knowledge puffs up!" But if you read it carefully, Paul says that "they do not yet know as they <u>ought</u> to know." In other words, they don't have <u>enough</u> knowledge yet! A little knowledge is dangerous, -- actually <u>more</u> knowledge will keep them from error.*

The Tools for teaching the Bible - The Bible

on a level of childishness, because they were a nation of drunks who ignored their prophets. In their drunkenness they mocked his solemn words! So, the Lord decides (verse 13) that they'll get more of what they gave him – nonsense (verse 11). In severe judgment, he will have the last laugh, so to speak, and rule them through a people whose speech will be nonsense to them.

This is what I mean by slowing way down and carefully looking at what a passage actually says – instead of running away with hasty but incorrect conclusions.

- ***Don't be afraid of what it says*** – The Bible is the *truth*, and it's the *only* and *best* way to say the truth. You needn't be afraid of what it says or how it says things. God knows far better than we do about what's going on; we have to learn to listen for a change and let his Word speak to us.

  For example, when the Bible describes the unconverted human heart in black colors, don't change it – believe it and teach it. A person has to see his heart in this way if he's going to be motivated to seek a Savior who can save the worst of sinners.

  When the Bible describes a full-scale miracle, believe it and teach it. I know that modern unbelievers try to talk us out of believing such incredible things; but unless God does the impossible (a truth that the Bible teaches over and over again) we have no hope to solve our impossible problems. We need a power outside of this world to help us; we've tried long enough to do it the world's way – and failed for thousands of years – and now we want a God who can do what this world can't do. Miracles are a precious pillar in our life of faith.

Another important doctrine that the Bible teaches is Creation. Very few people believe what the Bible teaches about it; instead they believe some variation of modern evolutionary theory and physics. When they turn their backs on the Bible, however, thinking that modern man can't afford to be so naïve about the way the world really came into being, they're cutting themselves off from Israel's God. If you read through the Bible, you'll notice that the prophets, Jesus Christ himself, and the apostles all depended on the God who created the world *as Genesis describes it* for powerful solutions to their own problems. See for yourself. If you leave their company – even under the umbrella of modern science – you leave the company of faithful witnesses of God's works. Evolution can't help us; but miracles and commands of power and catastrophic judgments will build the kind of world that God wants to see.

> *There are three theories of Creation:*
> - *Genesis*
> - *Evolution*
> - *Theistic Evolution*
> *... and only one believes in miracles!*

> See these passages on what believers thought about Creation:
>
> 2 Kings 19:15
> Jeremiah 32:17-23
> Acts 4:24-31

- *Interpretive principles* – The Bible is a huge book, and very complex and confusing to the new student. Unless you come up with some sort of plan of attack on how to study it, you will quickly get lost. Where does one start? How do I know how to read things in it? Am I right or wrong in how I'm reading it?

   First, start on basic truths of Christianity. If you understand the fundamentals, you can read the rest of the Bible and generally know what's going on – or at least you won't go far

The Tools for teaching the Bible - The Bible

wrong as long as you keep firmly in mind what you do believe in.

Second, hopefully you'll work on the Ten Keys and master them. These will quite literally open up amazing insights wherever you work in the Bible. After a while you will get so used to thinking in terms of the Keys that they'll become second nature to you. You'll be able to see what a passage is talking about even when others are confused by it.

Third, you will probably develop a method of study of your own – a schedule, a procedure, an outline – something that you will take again and again to the Bible whenever you open it for study. If it works – if it helps you get insight into the Word and lets you see the glory of God in Christ – then by all means use it and rely on it. Useful devices like these and others are part of the "toolkit" of serious students and should be relied on.

- *Pass on your mastery* – The goal of the teacher of the Bible is to make students able to study the Bible *on their own*. I have no time for teachers or preachers who keep their people befuddled enough that they're helpless with the Bible, and rely on *them* for oracles from God. In God's eyes we are all priests, with the responsibilities of the new Temple on our shoulders. We *all* need to be familiar with God's voice in the Bible, because we all have spiritual duties to carry out that require wisdom from the Bible.

Leaders who trained followers –

Moses - Joshua
David - Solomon
Elijah - Elisha
Jesus –
Apostles
Paul - Timothy

The Tools for teaching the Bible - The Bible

"And the things you have heard me say in the presence of many witnesses entrust to reliable men who will also be qualified to teach others." (2 Timothy 1:2)

So, share what you've learned. Think about how you go about studying the Bible, and help your students walk through the same steps. This will require some thought, because many things we do are second nature to us and hard to explain to others. It's like driving a car: at first we might think that it would be easy to explain it to someone. But when we get our teenager behind the wheel, we find to our amazement that they can't understand our simplest instructions! The problem may be, however, that we have to rethink our strategy and make it simpler.

Use your own methods and break them down, step by step, like an instruction book. Go over it with the students until they can do it as well as you can. Help them walk through the steps until they can do it on their own. It's one of my greatest pleasures of life to see students work through a passage on their own, using a method that I taught them, and coming up with insights – often things I didn't even catch! That joy makes teaching the Bible worth it all.

The goal is to produce Christians who are "workmen ... who correctly handle the Word of truth." (2 Timothy 2:15) The needs of the modern Church are great; we need thinkers, people who can study, Christians who have learned the truth and can keep learning to meet the needs. We can't all continue to be fed like helpless babies by people who may or may not know what they're doing themselves – or worse yet, who may be trying to deceive the elect. (Matthew 24:24)

The Tools for teaching the Bible - The Bible

> *Sometime you ought to look through a copy of the <u>Mishnah</u> or the <u>Talmud</u> – both Jewish holy books – to get a sense of the fanatical argumentative nature of the Jews.*

- *Don't fall under Jesus' judgment of the Jews* – The Jews were experts on the Old Testament. They knew it far better than we know even the New Testament. And they knew it in Hebrew! So naturally they were offended when Jesus told them that they really didn't understand it *at all*.

They knew the text, they knew the superficial interpretations of passages, but they didn't know the root meaning of the Bible. They committed all the errors of interpretation that I've been warning you about. When they approached it in their own way, what they ended up with was a ridiculous mess that dishonored the God who wrote the Bible. Jesus not only was amazed how wrong they were, he rebuked them for their bad Bible study – the way they approached it made it certain that they would come up with *the wrong answers*:

You have never heard his voice nor seen his form, nor does his Word dwell in you, for you do not believe the one he sent. You diligently study the Scriptures because you think that by them you possess eternal life. These are the Scriptures that testify about me, yet you refuse to come to me to have life. (John. 5:37-40)

In another place he rebukes the Sadducees not for avoiding Bible study, but getting *wrong answers* when they studied it –

The Tools for teaching the Bible - The Bible

You are in error because you do not know the Scriptures or the power of God. (Matthew 22:29)

How should that make us feel, who hardly know the Bible at all in comparison to the learned Jews! It's necessary to study the Bible; but just studying it isn't enough. We have to study it in the *right way* – so that we come up with the *right answers* (God's answers).

A Method

A good teacher has a method in order to teach. A method is a plan of attack, an idea of where you want to go and how to go about getting there. It's the "road map" that guides the teacher in the right direction to make sure he/she and the students arrive at the goal – educated minds.

"... be transformed by the renewing of your mind." (Romans 12:2)

What I consider the fundamental approach to teaching – the first principle of good method in teaching the Bible – is the traditional teacher/student model. In other words, the teacher comes prepared with a certain amount of material, with the intent of *getting it into the minds of the students*. No other method comes close to producing the results that the Lord wants to see in his children. It's a time-honored method, and it's the method that most of his servants in the past used on their students, not the least being Jesus Christ himself.

There are at least two kinds of teachers: those who facilitate, and those who lead. The facilitators help the students find their own way through the material. They do it with "discovery" sessions, discussions,

The Tools for teaching the Bible - A Method

student exploration, and all the methodology that supports that approach.

The leaders, however, make the assumption that they know something about their subject and their goal is to get that information into the minds of their students. When it comes to teaching the Bible, this method is all-important. Teachers deal with the *truth* when they handle the Bible – not opinions, feelings, experiments, guesses, options, or whatever else modern teaching methods emphasize. God said these words and had them written down for us to learn, not to reject or play with. I know that the current trend is to approach Bible study in the "discovery" way just as we do other subjects in school, but I have to disagree with their method for the most part. Our job, as teachers, is to make sure our students *learn* this material and get it right.

Discussion Method

Leader Method

Discussion is helpful in its place, and necessary at times to get people thinking and expressing themselves in a group. But unless it's based on a real teacher-to-student flow of information, it's only going to be "pooling our ignorance" – sharing one's opinions and feelings about a subject that we don't know anything

The Tools for teaching the Bible - A Method

about. It's much the same effect as having discussion groups on calculus! Where would we get if we approached the sciences like that? There just has to be a time of intensive teaching, learning, memorizing, reciting, and testing to see if the necessary foundation of information is getting into our world view.

Aside from this first step of taking a direct approach to presenting the Biblical information, there are other aspects to good method in Bible teaching that you should learn to cultivate:

Presentation: people remember pictures.

People remember best what they can see. If you've ever noticed yourself looking at the pictures in a book before you start reading the text, you'll know what I mean. Advertisers know this, and they spend a lot of time and money putting pictures in their ads in order to catch your attention and make their point. And children aren't the only ones attracted to pictures! The human mind is naturally designed to focus on what we see, and pictures are easier to grasp than a lot of cold text.

But there are many ways to "paint a picture." Of course you can use some sort of graphics to make a point, but you can also tell a story in such a way that a very realistic picture forms in the minds of your students. If you tell the story as if all of you are there, watching the details unfold and sharing in the drama, they will remember it long after the dull sessions of memorizing passages.

Examples from personal experience are another graphic way of making your point. I remember in Hebrew class when my instructor was trying to explain to us how to pronounce one of the more difficult Hebrew letters. He said it sounded like the noise a camel makes when it groans. He knew, because he used to teach English in the Middle East and got very familiar with camels! I've never forgotten his funny demonstration in class as he imitated a camel groaning.

The Bible is full of pictures. The Old Testament naturally lends itself to this kind of presentation, and most of the New Testament – even though there are some heavy doctrinal sections – also follows a pictorial scheme. The reason is that our faith is based on a God who worked through historical events. So if this is the way God presented it to us, let's take advantage of its structure and pass it on to our students with its rich imagery and exciting history intact.

One point at a time. A cardinal sin that too many teachers (and preachers!) commit is to try to cover too much at once. They seem to think that they have to get everything into one lesson, since it all fits together; but actually they end up accomplishing almost nothing. There's such a thing as information overload.

Professionals have noted that the human mind can only take in so much. The saying is that we remember –

The Tools for teaching the Bible - A Method

**10% of what we hear,
50% of what we see,
90% of what we do.**

That can be really discouraging, especially if our style of teaching depends heavily on verbal instruction! We may as well assume that our students will forget, or didn't even get, at least 90% of what we said – no matter how important we thought it was!

> *What put me onto this was a book by Pastor David Mains, <u>Full Circle</u>. He asked his Sunday School Class what they thought he said in his sermon – and none of them heard what <u>he</u> thought he said! He changed his way of preaching as a result.*

The best thing to do is to sit down beforehand and write a summary statement of our lesson – a single sentence that sums up the point that we want to make. Not three points, not nine points, but **only one point**. Force yourself to prune your subject down to one point. You'll have the chance to cover other points later in class; supposedly your students will keep coming back. Don't risk your students missing everything just because you were too impatient to slow down and give them at least one thing well!

Then craft your entire lesson around that one point. Make the examples illustrate it, the parallel passages reinforce it, the questions you ask enlarge it and make it clearer. What you are after is this: when the lesson is over, any of your students will be able to tell you, when asked, what your point was. If they can do that, you've accomplished a great deal. If they can't, go back and try again – you weren't making yourself clear.

The Tools for teaching the Bible - A Method

> *If you have a lot of material that you really want them to get, make up a handout and give it to them to take home and study.*

This requires some humility on your part. It's a shame that more preachers don't practice this method. It would no doubt be a revelation to them to find out that their hearers heard many different things, none of which match what the preacher thought he said! This teaching method of a single clear point is one of the toughest things to accomplish in teaching (especially for those who love to talk!). A classroom session is a one-shot opportunity. You only have your students a short time to get something to stick in their minds – and then they're gone. But it can be done; for those who master the technique, it makes the difference between a so-so teacher and a master of the art.

Repeat things. People usually don't remember something the first time they hear it. In fact, they remember little of what they hear, as we've seen above. The trouble is that we rely mostly on telling things to our students; the structure of a classroom is set up along the lines of *verbal* communication. So right away we're making things difficult on ourselves as teachers.

So you ought to find ways to take the *one point* of your lesson and say it in different ways. This will be easier to do if you *do* keep it to one point! If you have a lot of points in a lesson, you may as well forget about anybody remembering what you taught about. It's difficult enough to remember what a teacher said, without complicating it with trying to remember the *ten* points that the teacher covered in one class!

There are different ways of repeating your point. For example, you can start out with a pointed question – something that will lead naturally into your lesson, and something that will interest your students and get them to thinking. All your pictures can emphasize the point that your lesson is on. Getting the students to search for passages that support or explain your point is another way of repeating it. A session on how to apply your point is another way. All these devices will emphasize your point, and do it often – and yet they come at it *in different ways* so that it doesn't get tedious.

Show them God. If you don't master anything else in the art of teaching, you have to keep in mind the whole point of your teaching: your aim is to *teach your students about God*. That is so important, and yet it's usually the one grievous crime that teachers commit against the Word of God. The results are disastrous.

The Bible is about God. If you see that, you will become a master teacher and people will hang on your every word. We already have libraries full of books on other subjects – math, psychology, economics, history, politics, science, and on the list goes. But there is only one Book in which we can learn the truth about the true God – his Book, the Bible.

The Tools for teaching the Bible - A Method

> *C.H. Spurgeon, a famous London Baptist preacher of last century, once said that the whole Bible reveals Christ. If he preached on a verse that didn't specifically mention Christ, he would "jump the fence" to the verse beside it and pull him back over!*

Here we find an amazingly simple and yet astonishingly complex picture of who God is and what he does.

When you read the Bible, don't make the mistake that many make – they look for themselves in its pages, or wisdom on subjects that they're interested in researching. Look and study until you see God there. He is everywhere in its pages; he's the point of the story, the plot, the primary Agent of all its history, the Creator of the world it describes and the One for whom it was all made. Take God out of the Bible and you have, essentially, nothing meaningful left. This will take practice, and forcing yourself into a disciplined kind of study – it's not always obvious what the text is saying about God, especially when we're so used to seeing ourselves there instead. Pray about this and God will reward you: the revelation of God will begin to wash over you as you sit at his feet here.

Then take that information back to your students and give them God. They don't need wise sayings, or "do this and do that" as so many false religions try to give us. They need the news of a God who saves, who made everything for his purposes, the God who does miracles, the God who hates sin and loves and rewards righteousness. They need a clear picture of who this God is, and everything he did, so that they will have a good reason to put their own hope in him for the same things. Do this for them and you are literally offering them salvation; give

"He must become greater, I must become less."
(John 3:30)

The Tools for teaching the Bible - A Method

them less than God, and you're denying them life. In other words, whether they live or die in God's Kingdom may just rest in your hands – and you will prove yourself the faithful servant if you refuse to take glory to yourself, if you instead direct their eyes and minds to the God who can save them from sin and death.

Make them think. Rote memory is good, because it puts the material in students' minds in a way that they can bring it back from memory at will when they need it. But memorizing Scripture is only the first step to mastering it. If we stop there, we haven't accomplished much. What we want to do is to push people into thinking about the Bible.

The Bible was *made* to think about. It's the wisdom of God; it's the explanation of the nature of God and all of his works for mankind. It's the window into God's eternal world where we will see the answers to satisfy our restless minds. God didn't have to tell us any of this; he could have left us in the dark about the world of mystery behind our physical universe. But he chose to reveal it to us in the Bible – and those who care to explore it will find a depth there that no other subject can match.

But people don't like to think. As we will see below, thinking requires mental effort, and most people in our "entertainment" culture are too lazy to think – even about the most important issues of life! You have to steel yourself to their inevitable objections and *make* them think about the Bible.

How do you make your students think? **First,** take them to the actual passage that you're studying and let them read it, or listen to it. In other words, get all the information out before them. The human mind likes to see all the facts out in the open if it's expected to make sense of everything.

Second, don't ask questions that have the answers already in them. In other words, try to avoid leading questions. For example, you could be teaching the passage in Matthew 4 about Jesus calling his disciples; if you ask your students, "who did Jesus call to be his disciples?" – that's a leading question, and you'll only find out who can read the answer in the text. Ask them *why* Jesus called them, however, and you'll start getting furrowed brows, scratched heads, and the beginning of some creative answers – you'll see the process of thought at work.

Third, help them think it out by asking the right questions. What I mean by that is this: you have to know beforehand where you're headed with your lesson. If you don't know yourself what the passage is talking about, you can't very well help others see its point. If you know where things have to go, you can lead them along the right road, much like leading a group of tourists from point A to point B to point C – progressing along the right path so that everyone will see

The Tools for teaching the Bible - A Method

the entire site. After all, supposedly you've already walked this path – your students want your informed insight, your experience, and your guiding hand toward the goal so that they can see it too.

With authority: not like the scribes. When you teach, do it with authority. There are those who don't like my style of teaching, because when I teach what the Word of God says, I don't allow any room for doubting it or "fixing" it with someone else's opinions. This is what God said; our only option is to accept it and believe it as it stands.

> *See Matthew 22:23-28 for an example of what the Sadducees found time to argue about.*

When the scribes taught, they shared their "opinions" with the group and invited discussion. The Jews loved debates, and they spent centuries arguing over fine points of the Law. The problem was that they didn't consider anybody's word on the Bible as final – even their greatest teachers presented their lessons as "theories" that had to stand the test of time before passing into history as dependable.

> *"He taught them as one who had authority, and not as their teachers of the Law."*
> *(Matthew 7:29)*

But Jesus rejected this methodology. "You are in error because you do not know the Scriptures or the power of God." (Matthew 22:29). There are just some things that aren't a matter of opinion! Don't be apologetic about the truth. Christ came into this world to show us the *truth*; he died to give it to the Church – all of us. He sent out his apostles with the message of truth – that means that our Bibles are the revelation of God in Christ, the truth, the clear presentation of who God really is and what he does to and for mankind. If we believe it, we will be saved; if we doubt it or change it or reject it, we will be lost. There is no room for debate here.

It's the same thing as if a drowning man were thrown a lifesaver. This is no game: grab the thing and hang on! Jesus came to rescue the perishing; he didn't come to save the "righteous" but sinners. He came so that we may have life, not death. The claims are in the Bible that it's the urgent truth, that we must not argue with it but believe what it says. Only the perverse would turn it into a forum of opinion and debate. Notice what the philosophers of Athens did with it – Acts 17. They got no salvation until they believed it.

So when you teach, don't apologize about the Bible. Present it as if you believe it yourself. Hopefully you love your students enough to give them this precious Word of life that will save them if they believe it too. Declare the truth boldly, as the apostle Paul so often did himself. Don't worry about whether people will ridicule you, or reject what you're saying. Your job isn't to convince them of the truth (that's the Holy Spirit's job) but to present the truth as God gave it to you. Leave the rest in God's hands. If you do that, with boldness, with faith, with no fear or doubts yourself, God will honor your efforts.

The Tools for teaching the Bible - A Method

Of course, you understand that you have to know the truth yourself before you so boldly declare it to others. Many half-truths and outright foolish ideas have been taught in the name of Jesus! He will only own *his* truth, not your version of it. You have to know what you're talking about first. That's why James warns us that we who are teachers ought to be careful, because we're going to be judged more strictly. (James 3:1) Preach the *truth* boldly, and you'll be helping to build God's kingdom; preach lies and half-truths boldly, and the only kingdom that you'll be helping to build is the enemy's.

Testimony. Most people little realize the power and importance of a witness. In a court of law, a witness can make or break a case. Everything literally depends on his testimony. No matter what physical evidence has been presented, if the witness without hesitation claims to have seen the event, the court proceeds with his testimony and forms its verdict.

"Since we are surrounded by such a great cloud of witnesses ..."
(Hebrews 12:1)

The entire Bible is actually a collection of affidavits from countless witnesses of God and his works. God designed the Bible like this for a good reason: we cannot reject the testimony of an eyewitness. If someone says that they saw God, or saw God in action, how can we doubt an eyewitness? What argument can we present that would prove him wrong? Who are we to reject the testimony of someone who was there and actually saw what happened? God's method here was wise beyond understanding.

We could expand this idea much further in respect to the Bible, but we'll switch gears here and make the same point in respect to the teacher. *Teach what you know, and what you have experienced for yourself.* A testimony to what God has done in your life is unarguable. It will stop any and all arguments. Unbelievers can't deny what you've experienced without calling you a liar – and it's doubtful that they would go that far. You have one of the most powerful spiritual weapons in God's arsenal when you testify to others about the truth you know about personally, because of the way you experienced it in your life.

This again requires that you have meditated on God's Word, that you have learned it and understood it to its depths, that you have mastered how to apply it in your own life and you've been experiencing the benefits of its truth. Really, an inexperienced teacher is a pitiful creature (heed Paul's warning about the newly-converted doing the teaching in the church – 1 Timothy 3:6), because people have good reason to doubt his words. If he hasn't found out for himself how true the Bible is and how useful it is to God's people in their daily life, how can he expect others to believe in it? But an experienced Christian, one who knows how to listen to God in the

The Tools for teaching the Bible - A Method

Word, and who has walked with him according to that Word, has something authoritative to say to others. His experienced wisdom is both difficult to refute and very appealing.

In summary, the teacher of the Bible needs to know his/her textbook thoroughly. I hate to say this, but most people who try to teach the Bible don't know themselves what it's talking about. I've seen well-meaning "teachers" struggle with a Bible lesson – they usually lean on a crutch like a Sunday School quarterly because they don't know how to create a lesson of their own – and resort to discussion instead of teaching. They hope by this "method" to make everyone feel a part of the process and feel that everyone has "learned" something. The trouble is that if our schools depended on such a method, we would have a pitiful bunch of students at graduation – they would know next to nothing unless they learned to get it on their own! Certainly the teachers would have been of no help to them.

But we do that all the time in the Church. Instead of taking such a lame approach to educating God's people in the Word, however, we need to find teachers who can learn the material for themselves. And we need those who can be trained to pass on that information to other students in the most effective and God-honoring manner. It's time that we brought the Church up to speed on powerful teaching methods.

Bible Study Helps

There are other tools of the trade that the Bible teacher would do well to get and learn how to use.

The Tools for teaching the Bible - Bible Study Helps

These are sort of "back-stage" tools, tools that you would use in preparation for a class and not necessarily during class. It's a good idea to get as familiar with your subject as you can, and these tools help expand the horizon on your subject and clear up some mysteries.

A Concordance – A concordance is a book containing all the words that are used in the Bible, in alphabetical order, with the references where each word can be found. For example, if you wanted to know all the places in the Bible where the word "sheep" is found, you would look up under the entry "sheep" and probably see something like this:

SHEEP		
Ge 12:16	and Abram acquired s and cattle,	7366
20:14	Then Abimelech brought s and cattle	7366
21:27	So Abraham brought s and cattle	7366
24:35	He has given him s and cattle,	7366

Notice that it gives not only the references, but a little bit of the context of that verse – so that you can tell at a glance whether this is the reference you are looking for.

There are concordances for most of the major Bible translations available: for those who use the King James Version, there is ***Strong's Exhaustive Concordance*** and ***Young's Concordance***. For the NIV lovers, there is the ***Exhaustive NIV Concordance***.

In the back of both Strong's and the NIV Concordances, there are two dictionaries – one for Hebrew and one for Greek. These dictionaries list every single Hebrew and

The Tools for teaching the Bible - Bible Study Helps

Greek word that the original Bible uses, along with a short definition of each word. Notice too that each word is numbered. These are the numbers that you see in the main body of the Concordance, right after the short context line. If the number is italicized in the Concordance, that means that you can find it in the Greek dictionary in the back; if not italicized, then it's in the Hebrew dictionary. These dictionaries can be very helpful to you as you try to figure out what the original Bible actually said (which isn't always what a modern translation will give you!)

A Bible dictionary – A Bible dictionary is an encyclopedic reference for the *subjects* of the Bible. It has many articles about not only the history of the Bible, but its culture, geography, the nations that surrounded Israel, its languages, money used, customs, archaeological discoveries, and so on. A good Bible dictionary is great fun to read through. And it will have many pictures of what it describes so that you can get a better idea of these strange, obscure things you read about in Scripture. It will help you "paint the picture" more easily for your students.

> *Check out Zondervan's Bible Dictionary.*

Nave's Topical Bible – Nave's is a handy book to have. It lists all the topics found in the Bible in alphabetical order. Under each topic heading, you will find all the Bible passages that discuss any aspect of that topic – usually with the passages printed out in full.

In other words, if you wanted to look up the subject of **love**, leaf through Nave's until you find the topic "love." Under that you will find the passages on **love** starting with Exodus 20:6, then Deuteronomy 6:5, and so on. Since it prints out the actual passages, the topic covers 10 pages in Nave's!

Be aware that Nave's catches *almost* all the topics of the Bible. I found one that it doesn't cover – a significant one, I was surprised it wasn't included, seeing how extensive a topic it is in the Bible. But for the most part this is the book you will spend time in when developing lessons around particular subjects.

Greek-Hebrew helps – The Bible was first written in three other languages – the Old Testament in Hebrew and a little bit of Aramaic, and the New Testament in Greek. But because civilizations since then have chosen to speak in their own languages, we have always had the need to translate the Bible from the original languages into our own mother tongues.

Just as a sample, here are a couple of passages in the original languages:

בְּרֵאשִׁית בָּרָא אֱלֹהִים אֵת הַשָּׁמַיִם וְאֵת הָאָרֶץ:

This is the first verse of the Bible – Genesis 1:1 – in Hebrew. It's the language that Moses and all the Prophets wrote their books in.

Ἐν ἀρχῇ ἦν ὁ λόγος, καὶ ὁ λόγος ἦν πρὸς τὸν θεόν,

The Tools for teaching the Bible - Bible Study Helps

καὶ θεὸς ἦν ὁ λόγος.

And this is the first verse of the Gospel of John, written in Greek. All the New Testament writers wrote their books in Greek.

But you don't have to know Greek or Hebrew in order to teach the Bible. In God's wisdom, we have adequate modern translations that do a fine job in getting the true meaning of the Bible into our own language. We have everything we need for faith and practice in our English Bibles.

But translation is a tricky business at best. Sometimes the translators can't do much with a word or phrase because it's either difficult to put into modern English, or the original manuscript seems to have a problem. In cases like that, it isn't a bad idea to know how to work with Greek (and perhaps Hebrew) words so that you can do some exploration of your own. At least you ought to know what the resources are.

- We mentioned above that both Strong's and the NIV Concordances have Hebrew and Greek dictionaries in the back. Because of their numbering system, they are keyed to the main Concordance to give you an idea of what original word is behind the English word that is used in a passage. That's a good start.

The Tools for teaching the Bible - Bible Study Helps

> *Did you know that Jesus and Peter meant two different things when each used the word "love" in the passage John 21:15-17? John shows us in the Greek!*

- Second, you really ought to go out and buy a copy of *Vine's Expository Dictionary*. It has all the important Greek words of the New Testament in it – and discusses the depth of their meaning in a way that you could never know by just reading the Biblical passage itself. For instance, you will get an extensive discussion there between the three Greek words *agape, phileo,* and *eros* – all of which are translated as "love" in English.

   Unless you really love languages, I wouldn't necessarily recommend learning Greek or Hebrew. It's time consuming, and learning a language can be difficult for most people. Besides, most of what you'd learn in a grammar you probably won't use in normal Bible study. The most you would use Greek or Hebrew for is the meaning of a word that a simple translation can't get across for us.

- *An Atlas* – It really helps to know something about the geography of the Bible lands. You may not think so at first, but an atlas can change a cold, uninteresting account into a real-life story involving real people. These stories that the Bible records for us actually happened in history, in a particular place on earth; knowing what that place is like goes a long way to helping us see the whole picture behind the story.

For example, the story of the Good Samaritan takes on some additional reality when you actually travel that road between Jerusalem and Jericho. Jerusalem sits up on the mountains of Israel – it's part of a mountain chain that runs like a backbone, north and south, through the entire country. From right outside Jerusalem, toward the east, you can look down and see the valley where the Jordan River runs north and south; you can even see the northern end of the Dead Sea. There's a road there, starting at the top of the mountain ridge, that winds down along the side of the mountain, until it comes out at the bottom in that Jordan valley and goes on to Jericho near the river. In Bible days this road was, of course, unprotected; there were many possible hideouts for robbers among the rocks and ravines of a rough mountain road. A traveler felt alone and exposed to any danger along the way, and naturally could hope for no help if attacked. If someone did happen along and find a man beaten along the road, to leave him there was to leave him to his death. Doesn't this add depth to the story?

I would recommend Barry Beitzel's excellent *Moody Atlas of Bible Lands*. It's the best one I've seen. It not only gives you excellent maps showing the Middle East and Israel in different eras of history, it carefully describes the geography of the Middle East and how it had an impact on key Bible stories. It also follows the story line by means of historical descriptions of peoples and nations in the Middle East.

The Tools for teaching the Bible - Bible Study Helps

Bible versions – You can get a lot of insight into what the original version actually said – in other words, the actual Hebrew manuscript that Moses wrote, or the Greek letters that Paul wrote – by comparing different English Bible versions. Since most of us aren't going to learn Greek and Hebrew, we have to have some way of making up the loss. This is one effective way.

As was mentioned above, there is no way that a translator – even a good one – can get the entire meaning of the original over to English. He just has to do the best he can and say in English what he feels the Hebrew and Greek is trying to say. But as Proverbs mentions, there is wisdom in consulting many counselors. There have been several good translations of the Bible over the years, and we can take advantage of that in our study.

The Greek and Hebrew manuscripts come from a different world than ours, and there are many truths in the original that need to come out – and one version can't do the whole job. So one translator will bring out one aspect, another will bring out a different truth, and so on. If we gather them all together we can form a more complete picture of what God is trying to communicate to us.

What you can do is check several versions and how they word the passage that you're studying. What you're looking for isn't the one that tickles your fancy the most, but an all-around sense of what the original must have said. Here's an example from John 1:5:

καὶ ἡ σκοτία αὐτὸ οὐ κατέλαβεν.

and the darkness could not (_____?) it.

The word κατέλαβεν is in the aorist tense, from καταλαμβανω which means to seize, grasp, comprehend, make one's own, overcome, overtake, catch, or understand. Now which meaning should we use here? Either the darkness couldn't do violence to the light, or it failed to overtake it, or it couldn't understand it. There is a lot of difference between these meanings! And they're all valid ways of translating the word. When you check your English versions, you will find that they each use a different translation of this word – which will give you a richer understanding of what this word means.

For another example, this passage in the Gospel of John is particularly difficult:

Τί ἐμοὶ καὶ σοί, γύναι;
What to me and to you, woman?

This is what Jesus said (literally!) to his mother at the wedding at Cana (John 2:4). It sounds so harsh to our modern English ears that no version will translate it literally. They all choose to translate it idiomatically, because they know that it has a meaning that you can't see by looking only at the literal words used. Here is how three different translations handle the idiom:

Dear woman, why do you involve me? (NIV)
Woman, what have I to do with thee? (KJV)

The Tools for teaching the Bible - Bible Study Helps

> *Modern English translations are based on the "eclectic" Greek text of the United Bible Societies (Aland and others), and the Hebrew Bible (edited by Kittel and others).*

You must not tell me what to do. (TEV)

They aren't being dishonest with the text. Translators know that, in order to faithfully represent the original Greek and Hebrew in English, they have to move over not only the actual words used but also the *way* that words are used together – which often results in a meaning that the individual words would never have led you to suspect. We call this feature of language an *idiom*. When we say, "I'm going to run down to the store," there are at least two things in that statement that we don't mean literally! So by checking different versions, you will learn how the translators struggled with the idioms of the original as well as the literal words.

I hope you realize that this is important – God didn't record his truth in English! We're at a disadvantage now, since we don't speak those ancient languages any more; but we have to do our best to "gather up the fragments" and hear what he has spoken to man.

For those who love the King James Version, just remember that English has undergone a tremendous amount of change since 1611. It's our obligation to our generation and those following to preserve the Bible not in the language of Shakespeare, but in the language in which people speak. The goal is to *understand* the Bible. The King James Version did that in its day, and now we have to carry the torch. There's nothing wrong with translating the Bible into today's English. Wycliffe, for example, translates the Bible every day into languages used around the world.

Commentaries – A commentary is what someone else thinks a Biblical passage means. The author will write his thoughts about a whole book of the Bible and get it published. The only difference between you and that author, in other words, is that he published his opinions and you haven't yet.

> *A good – but old English – commentary is Matthew Henry's Commentary, 6 volumes. It's definitely worth having.*

That may sound a bit harsh, but actually it's true. Commentators are usually distinguished scholars who supposedly know what they're talking about, but I've seen many commentaries that obviously didn't have a clue about what the Bible teaches. I only take the good ones half seriously, and even then only if they are friendly to my overall attitude to the Bible itself. Besides, usually there isn't enough room to fully explore a Biblical passage in a page or two of commentary; simply because of space constraints the commentator has to cut short his opinions and give us a superficial understanding of a bottomless well of truth.

What you have to learn to do is explore the passage on your own first. Don't touch that commentary until you're done studying! If you follow good sound principles of Bible study, you will find yourself opening all sorts of doors to the passage – asking and answering scores of questions, finding ties to other passages all over the Bible, uncovering applications and useable ideas. This is, in other words, fruit of your labor that the Lord has graciously given you.

The Tools for teaching the Bible - Bible Study Helps

When you've studied a passage to this kind of depth, going to a commentary can be sort of anti-climactic – especially when you see how little there is there, compared to what you yourself have come up with. Basically I use commentaries to do two things: **first**, to make sure I'm on the right track and not coming up with something that runs contrary to what the historic Church has taught about the Bible. I don't fancy starting my own cult based on mistaken notions from my Bible study! **Second**, I check to see if I'm missing anything. Commentators have studied this passage too, and they got their own insights from the Lord (supposedly! – not always, though – man's ingenuity often gets him into trouble). So I want to glean what he learned and fit it into my study to fill in the gaps.

Computerized tools – We have tools at our disposal that people in earlier history didn't have. Computers have opened up powerful opportunities for the Bible student that past students would have given their right arms to have.

There are Bible versions, Greek and Hebrew Bibles, Naves Topical Bible, Bible atlases, archaeological studies, theological books – all on computer. You can quickly spend a fortune on libraries of information! Although nothing will replace that solid feeling of handling an old-fashioned book, having it on computer will make searching for things an unbelievable breeze. Plus, whatever you find you can insert into your own productions and hand out to your students.

The Tools for teaching the Bible - Bible Study Helps

> *Check out Crosswalk on the Internet – it will give you hundreds of Christian sites to explore.*

The Internet is quickly becoming a resource of unbelievable proportions. One has to be careful about the Internet these days, though – our Wise Fathers who rule our nation have recently decreed that anybody with a perverse mind (i.e., porn sites) can throw their immoral wretchedness in front of us without warning (I wonder if they've thought about what the *results* of that "freedom" are going to be?). It's best to find those sites that are safe and stick to them, especially relying on the experience of others who know their way around. But in spite of the problems, one ought to use the power of this resource in one's studying; it's like a world-wide encyclopedia on virtually any subject you wish to explore – and it's almost all free.

Think

> *"Five percent of people can think; ten percent of the people only think that they can think; and eighty-five percent of the people would rather die than think!" (Thomas Edison)*

It may seem strange that one of the tools for teaching the Bible is to think. Unfortunately, many people don't like to think – it requires too much effort, and they don't see the need for it. We've been raised on so much entertainment in this generation that now it requires a great deal of effort to force ourselves to give something some concentrated thought.

But thinking deeply about the Bible pays rich dividends. People often ask me how I know so much about the Bible – my answer is that I have taken seriously what the Bible says about itself:

Blessed is the man [*whose*] delight is in the Law of the Lord, and on his Law he

The Tools for teaching the Bible - Think

meditates **day and night.
(Psalm 1:1-2)**

Christian meditation – unlike the Eastern variety – focuses on God and his Word. We especially must start with the Word of God, because it's here that we get the truth to focus our minds on. We are supposedly looking for the truth – other religions look out to the greater universe or the "inner light" for its truth, but we start with what God purposely gave us as truth. We've already accomplished what all other religions have failed to achieve as soon as we pick up the Book.

And when we look for God in his Word, we are using the Bible for what it was designed to do: reveal the nature and works of the true God. Again, other religions fail in their attempt at pursuing truth because they are looking for gods that aren't real. They didn't bother to get their facts straight, so it's no wonder that they're off looking in the dead-ends of the universe for a God whom they won't find. We, however, when we start with God's self-revelation, *will* find him – we will hear him speak to us here, and we will see him in his glory. We will discover the reality of our God because we start looking for him in the right place.

*"Run in such a way as to get the prize."
(1 Corinthians 9:24)*

Everyone can think; they just don't know they can. The mind needs to be exercised just like the muscles. People aren't used to thinking, so it hurts them and bothers them when you make them do it. It requires discipline, just as any other strenuous effort does. Don't be surprised, then, when your "lazy self" rebels at the effort! Just dig in, like an athlete training to win a prize, and work at it.

How does one think about the Bible? Fortunately there's a method to it; if you use this method, you'll avoid fruitless sessions of trying to harness a wandering mind.

The Tools for teaching the Bible - Think

First, *ask questions*. This is, without a doubt, the most effective way of getting you started on a passage. If you really work on this step, you can open up the text in an amazing way: all sorts of ideas will come to you. As you ask the questions, you will begin to see the true layout of the passage – you will begin to understand what's important in it, and where to do more study. Answers will begin to suggest themselves to you. You will start seeing connections with other passages that can illuminate this one. It's amazing how effective this approach can be.

> *Scientists use this same method to make discoveries in the natural world.*

For example, let's take a sample passage: Psalm 1.

> [1] Blessed is the man
>   who does not walk in the counsel of the wicked
> or stand in the way of sinners
>   or sit in the seat of mockers.
> [2] But his delight is in the law of the LORD,
>   and on his law he meditates day and night.
> [3] He is like a tree planted by streams of water,
>   which yields its fruit in season
> and whose leaf does not wither.
>   Whatever he does prospers.
>
> [4] Not so the wicked!
>   They are like chaff
>   that the wind blows away.
> [5] Therefore the wicked will not stand in the judgment,
>   nor sinners in the assembly of the righteous.
>
> [6] For the LORD watches over the way of the righteous,
>   but the way of the wicked will perish.

The Tools for teaching the Bible - Think

To the person who doesn't like to think, the meaning of the psalm is "obvious" (a typical response!) – a righteous person stays away from the wicked, and God blesses him for it. But let's ask some questions, because there is far more going on in this passage that we don't want to miss:

Why is the word "walk" associated with "counsel?" Or "stand" with "way of sinners?" Or "sit" with "seat of mockers?" Why are we "blessed" when we avoid each of these? What does "blessed" mean, anyway?

Why be "delighted" in the Law? I thought it was a burden to a sinner!

What does "meditate" mean? What will happen when I meditate on the Law? What will I see there when I probe into it like that? Does "day and night" mean "constantly on my mind?" How do I do that? Why is it necessary to do that? What will happen if I don't?

Will I, as a Christian, come up with something in my meditation on the Law that will be different from what a Jew finds?

Could it be that my present state of being spiritually "dry" comes from not meditating on the Law? It says that one who meditates on it will be like a tree planted by water – fresh leaves, seasonal fruit. What are the streams of water? Why does meditation put me close to them? What fruit does God want to see in me? Does the Law have anything to do with that? What does "wither" mean in a person's life? What would it be like to not "wither?" "Whatever he does prospers." Is that me? On what level is that always true for a Christian? Can we expect it in this world? Why is it that, when we are doing well spiritually, physically things have never been worse? Does that contradict this passage? Or is the Lord interested in different things than we are?

Well, I'll let you finish the psalm. Since I've already "meditated" on this Psalm a good bit in the past, I've come up with some surprising answers to these questions! What was supposedly a "well-known" passage turned into a well-spring of new possibilities for study. It's like digging a well: suddenly the water shows up and it won't quit!

The important thing to see is that a barrage of questions will "loosen up" the passage enough that you can begin to take it apart, and see what's really there beneath the surface.

Second, *spend time on a passage*. It's helpful to read through a passage to get its general drift, but you won't find its true depth unless you stop and dig in it a while. The Bible yields its treasures with effort on your part – and that takes time. It can't be done in a moment.

We don't like to spend time on anything because we like instant answers. If we can't get something in a hurry, we're not interested – we will willingly do without. But that's fatal, spiritually speaking, because we're doing without the *truth* when we hurry through the Bible. The Bible is like a field of blackberries: unless we're willing to stop and work a while, if we're satisfied to just run down the path and glance at things

The Tools for teaching the Bible - Think

on our way by, we won't end up with anything in our basket.

Spending time on a passage means coming back to it again and again. Don't stop digging with one or two readings. I've returned to a passage countless times, re-reading it, digging some more, tracking down a related passage that may help me understand the first one, and then weeks later coming back to it again. In fact, there are some passages I'm still going back to years after I first started studying them!

The reason you have to spend time on a passage is that there is almost always more there than you think there is. Don't be satisfied with a superficial understanding of a passage. Keep asking questions, and you will see that almost every passage in the Bible can be endless! There is, of course, a point at which you can stop and share what you've learned with others – just because you haven't plumbed the depths of a text yet doesn't mean that you aren't ready to teach it. But never close the book on anything you've already studied.

Perhaps the one reason that people don't think about the Bible is that it takes time to think, and we hate to spend time on something that requires effort. If we could understand it immediately, we would willingly spend the effort; but when it takes so much time and things don't fall into place right away, we quickly give up and move on to more interesting things. People who have achieved great things in life, however, will tell you that they first spend enormous amounts of time working on the preliminaries before the project started to fall into place for them.

Third, *don't assume anything!* Thinking is like driving in certain respects: some things can turn into roadblocks that keep you from moving forward. There are some

The Tools for teaching the Bible - Think

things that get in the way of thinking, and prevent you from seeing what is really there in a passage.

> *The Medieval world assumed that the Roman Catholics were right – and then Martin Luther came along!*

For example, we all make the mistake of assuming that everything we've heard in the past about a particular passage is the right way to look at it. If what we've heard is really true, then that's OK; but often people have told us things without having thought it out for themselves – and now we're in danger of sharing their ignorance.

Did you know, for instance, that *nowhere* in the New Testament did *anybody* end their prayer with the words, "in Jesus' Name, Amen" – even though the disciples were *specifically told* to pray "in Jesus' Name?" (John 16:24) Go ahead and look – it's not there. Could it be that our generation – which takes such care to use this phrase at the end of almost every prayer – doesn't understand what Jesus was referring to? Did you know that nobody in the Church down through history ever used this formula until we Christians in the twentieth century did? Could that be the reason that we get so few answers to our prayers, compared to the great times of revival and growth in the Church in times past? Didn't Jesus assure us that we *will* get what we ask for *if* we ask for it in his Name? What, then, does he mean by that?

Another roadblock to thinking: too often we assume that we know what a passage means, simply because we've studied it in the past. It's surprising, however, when we return to a familiar passage after a while, armed with knowledge from other studies, and find it opening up in new ways. It happens regularly to a thinking student of the Word.

Fourth, *compare and relate passages.* No verse stands on its own in isolation from the rest of the Bible. Everything fits together like a beautiful fabric. We can

The Tools for teaching the Bible - Think

see God's infinite wisdom in how complex yet how amazingly simple and unified the whole message of the Bible really is.

Actually you can use the unity of the Bible to your advantage. So many people have isolated their favorite passage and made it say whatever craziness they want to see in it, with no regard to the fact that other passages contradict their opinion! For example, one of my favorites is the story of Lot. Most people (preachers and teachers included!) consider Lot to be a scoundrel, guilty of every crime in the book. This is in spite of the fact that Peter gives us a glowing account of his righteousness! (See 1 Peter 2:7-8) Things like that throw up red flags for me. Peter is always right, no matter what modern preachers might say to the contrary. When everyone contradicts the apostle so glibly, that makes me think that we don't understand the story of Lot as well as we think we do. Believe it or not, Peter is right – our traditional reading of the story of Lot is dead wrong. If we go back to the story with Peter's viewpoint, we can see a quite different scenario opening up there. In fact, once we really understand what's going on with Lot, we will wish we were as righteous as he!

"Lot ... a righteous ... righteous ... righteous man!"
(2 Peter 2:7-8)

By checking other passages that discuss the same idea as the passage you're studying, you will often find expanded explanations that will help you understand what you're studying. It's not often that a subject in the Bible is fully laid out for you in one spot only. Only by going to different places and gathering everything together will you be able to piece together the entire picture. If you don't do this, your students are easily going to find the holes in your understanding.

Finally, keep in mind that the point of learning God's Word is so that you can obey him and please him by what you learned. You will find a wealth of ideas of how to apply the truth of your text – by checking how other saints applied it in their lives. God's truth works, and there are millions of witnesses ready to testify to that fact. Use their experiences as learning material for yourself and your students.

Fifth, *get the real point, not the superficial point.* What I mean is this: it's too easy, when trying to figure out a passage from the Bible, to take the first idea that comes into your head and run with that. "It's obvious," people will say, when really there is much more depth to the passage than they realize. Of course they won't see it all unless they spend a great deal of time and thought on it; but some people don't want to put that kind of effort into it.

Actually God puts people off with the obvious. He purposely shrouded much of his truth in "mystery" – they may think they understand what he's doing, but really they have no idea. The Jews were often in a fog about God and his ways because he refused to reveal himself. And obviously by Jesus' day, the Jews were completely wrong about the Scriptures that they thought they understood. God protects his truth in this way from sinners who won't bend their knee in humility to him; they won't do things his way, so he hides himself from them – which means *no answers to prayer*.

But many Christians simply don't give the Bible a chance to unfold in its richness. For example, many students of the Word have interpreted the story of Isaac and Rebekah in Genesis 24 as simply a love story, an account of how believers ought to seek out other believers for marriage. Although that point is in the story, that's *not* the primary point of the passage. Once you get familiar with the Keys you will see several of them at work here: first, this is a story of **miracle** from beginning to end! It teaches the **ways** of the Lord, people living by **faith** in what they don't see but know is true, it brings **glory** to God who alone could have guided such a series of events, and it was part of the fulfillment of the **covenant** to Abraham. Limiting your study to how to go about getting married is ignoring the best parts of the story!

Another example: Christians often use the phrase "Jesus saves" without having put much thought into it. What does it mean that Jesus saves? Is it as simple as him dying on the cross and getting us forgiveness? If we would make a list of the steps behind that act of salvation, we would begin to see the magnitude, the tremendous scope and complexity behind this supposedly "simple" event:

- **Christ was crucified from the foundation of the world**
- **Promise to Adam and Eve, to overcome devil's work**
- **Covenant with Abraham, basis of all God's promises**
- **Patriarchs are the foundation of Israel**
- **Exodus from slavery in Egypt**
- **The Law – the description of a perfect Man**
- **Desert wanderings – learning God's Ways**
- **Conquest of Canaan – taking the Promised Land**
- **Judges – deliverance**
- **King David—model for the Messiah**
- **Temple – description of God's sacrifice**
- **Solomon – wisdom for living in God's Kingdom**
- **Exile & restoration – punishment & mercy**
- **Jesus' life, death, resurrection**
- **Ascension to Heaven – our home there**
- **Beginning of Church – sending the Spirit**
- **The Bible – revelation of God**
- **Present work of Christ's intercession**

As you can see, salvation was far from a simple matter! It took God thousands of years, working through millions of people, through a multitude of nations and complex historical events and processes, to get you into his Kingdom. So the next time you read

The Tools for teaching the Bible - Think

about "salvation" in the Bible, keep in mind the vast substructure lying behind the seemingly simple events in Jesus' life and work.

Here are some final points to consider about thinking:

- Being able to think will prepare you for applying the text for your students. We can all tell when someone doesn't understand what they're talking about, when they're just spouting off something they've memorized – like a Bible lesson. In fact, it's possible to memorize the entire Bible and not understand anything in it! But someone who has thought through the subject for themselves will be like a wise counselor – and I'll be able to get help from him on how to use the truth of the Bible.

- Don't be surprised if, after you've thought so much about Scripture, you lose everyone else! Remember that most people don't like to think. Just because they call themselves Christians doesn't mean that they've spent much time in Bible study – most don't. And when you try to discuss your study with them, they're going to look at you in the same way that a ten-year-old would look at a college student who's struggling with calculus! I don't mention this to make you proud; in fact, the more truth you see about God and Christ, the humbler you ought to become – that's a sign that you're getting the point! On the other hand,

"Every teacher of the Law who has been instructed about the Kingdom of Heaven is like the owner of a house who brings out of his storeroom new treasures as well as old."
(Matthew 13:52)

The Tools for teaching the Bible - Think

you need to be ready for the blank stares, the loneliness, the misunderstanding that you're going to run into from your friends who don't share your enthusiasm and knowledge. It's going to happen.

- It's been said that your goal in teaching is to know **ten times** more than what you will teach in class. This sounds pretty awesome, but I've found it to be a good general rule. If you barely know what you intend to teach about, it will be easy for your students to corner you and ask you related questions that you have no idea how to answer. On the other hand, if you're a master of your subject, you can pretty much handle whatever they might throw at you. Besides, you'll need to know how to apply the truth that you're teaching – and that means you'll inevitably be getting into unpredicted areas as your students want to know how to use what they've learned from you. (**Note:** keep in mind the "one point" rule. Even though you know much more about a subject, don't therefore dump it all out on the table! They will *not* be able to get it all, even though you desperately want them to. Just give them *one point* and then be ready for anything.)

- There is a good test for whether you really understand a passage the way you ought: when you can explain it clearly to someone else, so that they see what you see, then you know what you're talking about. You've no doubt

The Tools for teaching the Bible - Think

had the painful experience when you couldn't find the right words to express your thoughts, when your students looked at you blankly because you struggled to make something plain to them and failed. That's because you aren't ready yet to talk about that subject! You need to work on it some more, to think deeper about it, to find the right words, to make outlines, to hash it out in your mind and on paper, to do more research, and so on.

Judge The Results

Teaching the Bible can be an exhilarating experience. Many times I've come away from a teaching session rejoicing in the truth of God and how the Spirit helped me to deliver the message. Every teacher who loves his/her work aims for a job well done, and enjoying it is just icing on the cake.

"...his work will be shown for what it is, because the Day will bring it to light. It will be revealed with fire, and the fire will test the quality of each man's work."
(1 Corinthians 3:13)

But we have to be honest about this; reality has to set in sometime. We aren't working for ourselves – we are servants of the King, and we have to do the job to *his* satisfaction, not ours. He expects a profit on our labor, the kind of profit that he's looking for. That means that we have to ask ourselves a hard question after our teaching sessions:

Am I achieving my goal?

Remember what the goal is for a Bible teacher? **To get the Word of God into the minds of the students so that they know it and understand it.** We can't sit back and rest on our laurels until we find out if that's really the result of our teaching.

Judge the Results

Paul told the Corinthians that they were obligated to check themselves for results:

**Examine yourselves to see whether you are in the faith; test yourselves. Do you not realize that Christ Jesus is in you – unless, of course, you fail the test?
(2 Corinthians 13:5)**

This soul-searching is for a good reason: we can't afford mistakes. If we're working on a project and it's not turning out like it's supposed to, it's best to find that out before we finish it and walk away. While there's still time, we can take measure of what we've been doing and try to change our approach. If our teaching isn't accomplishing our goal, then we need to know that and find out what we're doing wrong. A construction worker may finish a hard day at work and be pleased with himself. But the question is, did he do his work according to the blueprints? If not, it has to be torn down and redone. Shoddy work will only ruin the overall plan.

Many teachers hate to ask themselves that question. They're afraid that they might uncover nasty surprises – like their students not remembering anything that was said! They hate to change what they do and how they do it (maybe out of pride). It would mean admitting their weaknesses, their ignorance, and going back to learn new techniques. Especially when someone has been teaching for a long time, it comes hard to admit that one has been doing it wrong for years.

But nobody is perfect; we can all learn new things – especially when the spiritual welfare of our students is at stake. For their sake, at least, we ought to be willing to look at what we're doing and try to improve. Surely we love them enough to do whatever we can to open wider the door to Life!

Judge the Results

If the student isn't living by the truth that he learned from you, then of course you're going to be distressed and moved to pray for him; what good teacher wouldn't? But whether he obeys God's Word is actually a matter between him and God; you can't *make* him obey it. The Spirit is the one who convicts, changes, and directs people in the way of life. All you can do is show him the way, not force him to walk in it.

Your job (and don't try to do the Spirit's job – it's impossible!) is to face the student with the Word so that they know and understand it very clearly. If your students are getting the point – if they can repeat key ideas back to you, and they understand those ideas because you made it simple and clear for them – then you've been doing *your* job. A teacher can expect no more for his/her efforts. Perhaps most of the frustrations in teaching arise from teachers trying to do God's work for him, instead of focusing on the part that they were given to do.

If they aren't getting the point, then you need to rethink your methods. Probably you aren't yet skilled at using your tools. Go back to each one of them and reexamine whether you understand the tool and how to use it. There's no shame in not fully knowing how to use these tools – they are *spiritual* tools and take some getting used to. People in more responsible positions than you have struggled with how best to use these powerful tools! And if you don't first succeed, try, try again. Persistence wins the war, not stunning first victories. Don't let pride be your downfall; admit to failure and weakness and ignorance, and work harder to improve.

As to how to determine how much the students are actually picking up, I'll let you work on that with creative methods. Some people use tests. Others use

Judge the Results

discussion sessions and listen carefully to what is said – often you can tell whether someone has been listening by the kinds of things they'll use to solve problems in group discussions. Or you can have personal counseling sessions with each student. There are many ways to find out what they've learned from you.

The important point is that you *need* to find out what they've learned. Don't let this opportunity slip away from you; this may be the last time that your students will hear the Word from someone who is so conscientious about their job.

Finally, the one thing that keeps us teachers going, in the middle of failures, hard-headed students, and a hostile world, is the Lord's promise that he will never let us go out and do this work on our own:

**All authority in Heaven and on earth has been given to me. Therefore go and make disciples of all nations, baptizing them in the Name of the Father and of the Son and of the Holy Spirit, and teaching them to obey everything I have commanded you. And surely I am with you always, to the very end of the age.
(Matthew 28:18-20)**

Notes

www.ingramcontent.com/pod-product-compliance
Lightning Source LLC
Chambersburg PA
CBHW020019050426

42450CB00005B/548